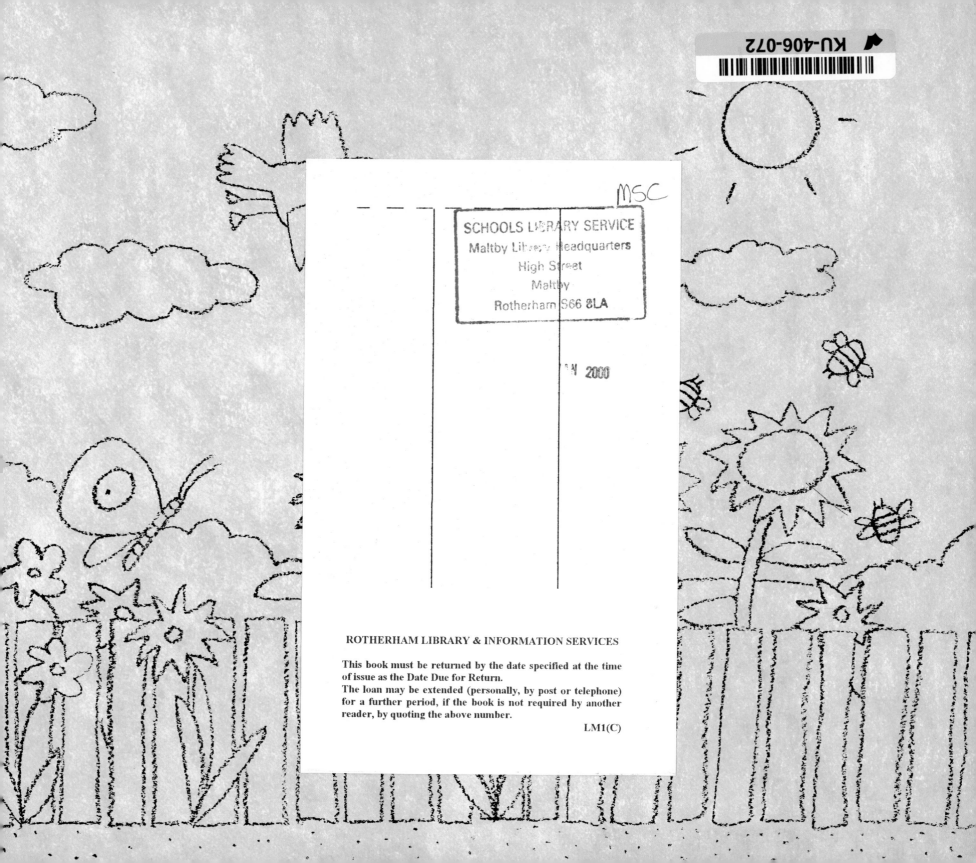

Eyes, Nose,

For the new gang –
Micha, Amira, Tristan,
Clarke, Matthew and Monica ~ J.H.

For Max ~ **B.G.**

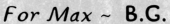
First published 1999 by Walker Books Ltd
87 Vauxhall Walk, London SE11 5HJ

10 9 8 7 6 5 4 3 2 1

Text © 1999 Judy Hindley
Illustrations © 1999 Brita Granström

This book has been typeset in Gararond.

Printed in Hong Kong

British Library Cataloguing in Publication Data
A catalogue record for this book is available
from the British Library.

ISBN 0-7445-2849-6

Fingers and Toes

A First Book About You

Judy Hindley

illustrated by
Brita Granström

WALKER BOOKS
AND SUBSIDIARIES
LONDON • BOSTON • SYDNEY

Eyes are to blink. Eyes are to wink.
Eyes are for looking and finding – **You!**
Eyes are to shut when you're asleep.
Eyes are for hiding ...

A nose is to blow.
A nose is to sniff.
A nose has holes
for sniffing with.

Ears are to find at
the sides of your head.
Are you wearing your
ears today?
Hurray!
Ears are to hear
a story with.

A mouth is to yawn ...
Open wide —
See all the teeth and the tongue inside?

A mouth is to laugh –
Ha-ha! Ha-ha!
A tongue is to talk
and to sing – La-la!
La-la,
la-la,
la-la!

Lips are to make

very small

for a kiss.

Lips are to whistle

and blow.

What about necks?
A neck is to tickle.
What about shoulders?
Those are to wriggle.

A back
is to
stretch
so high
and
tall.

A back is
to curl up
snug
and small.

Arms go up,

Arms go down.

Arms go reaching way out wide.
Arms can rock you side to side.

Hands are to hold and pat

and **clap!**

Hands are to hide behind your back.

Fingers and thumbs
are for counting on,
One,
two, three,
four,
five ...

And then,

six, seven, eight,
nine, ten.

Let's find some toes
and count up those —
And then
let's wiggle
and
waggle each one!

Legs are
for
leaping
and
jumping
and dancing.

and skipping
and hopping.

Legs are
for kicking

Knees are to bend,
    so let's all sit down —

BUMP! On our bottoms, side by side.

So here we are!
And I'll tell you again —
Kisses are little,

smiles are wide ...

A hug is a bundle
with YOU
inside.